The Quaker
Sonnets

Published by The Langley Press.

Simon is a Member of Northumbria Area Meeting of the Religious Society of Friends (Quakers)

Also From the Langley Press

Open House: A Quaker Tale in Verse by Simon Webb

Love Sonnets of Dante and His Contemporaries,
Translated by Dante Gabriel Rossetti

Chaucer's *Parliament of Fowls* in a
Modern Verse Translation

A Book of Quaker Poems, 1652-1900

The Theology of Small Things by Martyn Kelly

Poems in No Particular Order by Heather Cawte

Our Name is Legion: A Quaker Memoir of Depression
by Simon Webb

*Susannah's Sisters: Early Quaker Women and the Sects of
Seventeenth Century England* by Patricia Brown

For free downloads and more from the Langley Press,
please visit our website at: http://tinyurl.com/lpdirect

Contents

Introduction

These sonnets were written some twenty years ago, when I first became interested in the Quakers, and started attending Quaker Meetings for Worship. Although at the time I was reading up on Quaker history, I was rather neglecting the Quaker 'handbook', *Quaker Faith and Practice*. One of the most important elements of *Q F & P* is *Advices and Queries*, a set of questions and pieces of advice which sort-of stands in for a creed or catechism – something that the Quakers have never had.

At some point I decided to take *Advices and Queries* as the framework for a set of sonnets: I'd trained myself to write sonnets in the 1980s when I should have been studying harder for my English degree at Birmingham, and I thought it might be time to use this really quite useless skill.

How did I find the leisure to write forty-two sonnets? At the time, I was out of work and receiving benefits and treatment because of a mental collapse that had struck me down in 1996. There are oblique references to this situation in some of the sonnets below, which were partly written because the mental health professionals who were trying to untangle me suggested that I take up a hobby, and I knew that I'd always found writing therapeutic. The structure of the Shakespearian sonnet, which is both restricting and liberating, helped me to keep my wayward mind on the task.

The full story of how Quakerism helped me to return

to sanity is told in my book *Our Name is Legion.*

When I had finished the sonnets, I showed them to members of my local Meeting and others, and the response was positive, though several people suggested that I supply notes. The notes in this volume are new: I have put them at the end so as to avoid having footnotes on the pages that bear the sonnets themselves.

SW, June 2017

The Quaker
Sonnets

by

Simon Webb

1

Tell me, do you feel the same as me?
This gladness, sitting in the fifth-month sun,
With just one, half-forgotten enemy,
At peace within, without, with everyone?
I cannot help but think this end to pain
Is multiplied in those so heart-refreshed,
Although it's nearly nine, the sun must wane,
And light-freed images be night-enmeshed.
In dreams a rainbow light will soon depart,
Although the brain is shielded by its bone:
No light is seen in Mars's desert heart;
The light I see is not a ray alone:
Lightless, a dungeon and a womb are one,
And light unseen outshines the noonday sun.

2

His image so proliferates, I think
I'll never see a Jesus to revere.
In print, in pencil, or Renaissance ink,
Nothing can bring his mystery so near.
I wandered Florence in a fortnight's daze:
Great canvases looked out from every space;
A nimbus setting every head ablaze,
And tiny cracks of time in every face.
The sweeping steps of lovers in the street,
Or ancient, dusty, Tuscan farmer's hat,
Showed me much more of him, but also that
Old lady who knelt smiling at the feet
Of saints so saccharine they set the teeth on edge:
Yet, sweet transmitters of the Saviour's pledge.

3

I was baking, but my mind was not on bread:
It roamed far in the future, mined the past
And thought of 'if' and 'maybe' things instead.
(The bread was black and ruined at the last.)
Sometimes nostalgia wraps me in cool fire,
Often for things that were before my birth;
Or hectic speculation makes me tire
Of time, that goes round steady, like the earth.
But if I set out early on a walk
To Meeting, or a stroll into the town,
Alone, without the motive for tired talk;
My spirit rises and my pulse goes down:
I'm taken to that country, bound and free,
That loses time, and gains time's mystery.

4

Christ PLC's committee craned to hear
The ancient witness croak his dog-eared tale.
Though outwardly in serge, in coats of mail
Within, each listener noted a vague fear.
Men rising from the dead? Descents to Hell?
Blind people cured? The lame compelled to walk?
Ascending like pale smoke to Heaven as well?
Let's put an end to such old-fashioned talk!
As for the water-walking, it's absurd!
The sea was dry, and Jesus walked upon
The bottom - miracle is *not* the word!
(The witness, through the still-locked doors, is gone.)
To bear a footprint is not water's part:
Traces of Christ? For them, consult the heart.

5

Why did the walls of Jericho come down,
Yielding to tough Israeli minstrelsy?
Though wall-less, Durham is just such a town,
Ripe to be reconstructed utterly.
I like to picture Jesus in these streets
Dressed, like James Nayler, in an old brown suit;
Voice, booming cormorant and gentle flute,
Tipping sleek bishops from their splendid seats.
The Talmud's the yeshiva boy's delight;
The Qu'ran goes wherever the Muslim roams,
Its *suras* dwindling into cave-mouth light;
Sikh scripture sits above all other tomes.
If love for holy books has any place,
It lets us see, in them, our proper face.

6

My faith from desert, your faith comes from green.
Your god is female and has grass for hair -
Earth as a goddess, not a vast machine;
A forest clearing is her flowered chair.
My god is male and comes in fire and smoke -
He lights up wastelands as a hurtling star;
His people use dry camel-dung to stoke
Fires like bright flags, to spread his word afar.
Rank weeds kill flowers and trees are lightning-
felled,
And in such change I dimly strive to see
The ideal tree behind the stricken tree,
The tree that bearded Socrates beheld.
No, life does not fill all my inner sight:
Therefore my faith depends on inner light.

7

God, looking down through Galileo's scope,
Perceived bright stars within the master's head;
White glittering galaxies of thought and hope
Like sugared cakes on a black velvet bed.
The Italian's truth the pious wouldn't hear,
Removed us from the centre of all things
And freed the earth, gave the blue mother wings...
But no, that Saturn, truth, grew wings of fear
(While Muslim scientists scoured the desert skies
With shining astrolabes, and noted much
Our culture, priest-beset, was slow to touch).
This curiosity is no surprise;
The scientific paradigm now runs:
The stuff we're made of was born out of suns.

8

As Aaron's rod changed to a curving snake,
The roof-beam morphed into a copper-head.
The little girl who saw it tried to make
Her body still, despite her growing dread.
The prairie stretched around them, rusty-brown,
Where curious Vinland weeds attacked their wheat.
A Meeting-House, two farms, that made a town
For bitter struggles, and heart's concord sweet.
The snake observed their silence with sliced eyes
And fell into a first-day morning's doze;
The Friends glanced up with shivering surprise
And crept away, after the Meeting's close.
A Quaker legend, or The Quaker's Dream?
Fear faced with stillness, harmless as a beam.

9

The church was a converted old school hall,
A barn-like space, with lofty, curtained stage.
The people, as they shuffled in, were all
Or nearly all, of the mid-winter age.
The organ rattled with a wheezy breath:
The people sang strange hymns I'd never heard,
Of promised kingdoms, 'spirits' their key word:
This was a place where people worshipped death.
After the prologue/service was complete,
The medium mounted the high wooden dais,
A look of warm compassion on her face:
The dead seemed to come in, with loamy feet...
Though sitting in their midst, I sat apart
Nursing the one great spirit in my heart.

10

With chest puffed out, a man o' war's big sail,
Legs straight and springy, glasses raised by cheeks,
Hands clasped behind, like some glib royal male,
I flash pride's window and don't hear the creaks.
(At times, how little can inflate the mind:
A bus that comes, just as we join the long
Tired queue: an unexpected bookshop find,
A gentle wind, some trifle of this sort.)
Some people need a pint of port to get
This state of mind, that seems to scrape the sky;
The state that causes the true heart to die:
This Nayler knew, and his holed tongue speaks yet.
On heartbreak beach, some heaven is at hand:
A paradise to fill your boots with sand.

11

Just like the fiddler crab's (one small, one big)
Strange claws, that make him look so music-mad,
He totes a violin to play a jig
To his crustacean friends to make them glad,
So my strange hands, one normal and one small
Make me lopsided. My stooped-over back
Makes me forever seem to bear a pack
(A modest fault, well-known among the tall).
My wide, splayed feet, my disconcerting lope,
Side-pointing nose and eyes with their marked squint
Would make some melancholy men lose hope
Of worth, flawed coins rejected from the mint.
Perhaps this is my true, didactic fate:
To show all eyes the mind's imperfect state.

12

It said goodbye: the hostess closed the door.
A silence fell: all had been watching him,
The stranger some felt rich, and some thought poor.
Some found him fattish, others thought him slim.
 Some saw an old man, others would insist
A nun had spoken, her voice low and chaste.
Some saw a child, curly and open-faced:
Others saw Venus, ready to be kissed.
Some to uneasy beds, some to deep sleep,
The pious seekers rapidly dispersed.
Some words forgotten, others made to keep,
Still others uncreated, unrehearsed.
They'd asked round many notions in the past:
This had been Truth, the greatest and the last.

13

Listening to George Fox, some thought his speech
Came from the Bible, when it was not so.
Some thought his words his own when he would reach
Inside, to find a verse they didn't know.
The King James version (though described by some
As stiff and formal, beside Tyndale's wit),
Has words enough and space for everyone;
For generations it was holy writ.
I love the modern versions of the Book
And poetry (worth the name) of centuries.
Though ours, our words can still be enemies
To what lives in a tone, a pause, a look.
Like sky that swarms between two tall sunflowers,
The God that lives *between* the lines, is ours.

14

When it was mooted, people glanced around
To see what other folk like them might say.
A democratic vote took place to allay
All of their doubts, both petty and profound.
Musicians set the law to an old tune;
T-shirts were printed and worn everywhere.
It promised to release us from all care -
Pundits agreed it was bound to have happened soon.
Popular voices drowned attempts to plead:
The well-trained staff ensured all would go well.
Official witnesses beheld the deed.
So it was done, and the last silence fell.

15

Do you take part as often as you can
In meetings held for Quaker church affairs?
Are you a capable committee man
Or woman, able to sit long on chairs,
Plastic or wood, sponge-soft or coral-hard?
Can you bring wisdom to a tricky case,
And real concern, not just a caring face?
Can you be still, and wait for the trump card
In Quaker games, the quiet voice of God?
The voice that draws all disparate factions near
And makes the straining deaf delight to hear,
Soft as long hair, harder than any rod;
That rolls out like a new topgallant sail,
That stripes the clear sky like a vapour trail.

16

The Friends in Christ are small and little-known;
They're Quakers of an antique, Fritchley shade.
Against the tide of pluralists, they own
The Quakerism Fox and Nayler made.
They do not hesitate to plainly say
Christ is the object of their pilgrimage
And live apart on farms, and quite away
From the rainbow glitter of our latter age.
Again my words fall down beneath the weight
Of what I want to say: that this short day
Knows only what it can destroy, create,
And present things cannot be far away.
I have known mornings dance to an Attic tune,
And far futurity cut in at noon.

17

The sun would not shine on them, it became
A giant cymbal crashing in their heads.
Camels and men, they suffered all the same:
Hard-waking days, thin sleep on frozen beds.
Strange birds flew over them: the endless stones
Gave tiny dragons birth, when kicked aside.
Red kangaroos against the land's red tones
Gave joeys a long-footed, loping ride.
Though red themselves in parts, above bleached beards,
They cursed the 'roos and the weird natives too;
Though crusty, they despised these people who
Sat dust-besmeared and ate strange, filthy roots.
(The rocks sucked in the white men and their rage:
The Dreamtime wrote itself on the land's page.)

18

The lonely Hierophant sits on his throne
Under a cone-like crown with jewelled points:
Apostate hierarchy is the tone
Of this fifth card. The Lord I know anoints
Not hierophants alone, or bearded kings,
Prophets or ministers, or protestants
Or wayside Micahs who fume, scream and rant,
But everyone, and the billion living things.
The Hermit is depicted in a bare
Desert. He wears a dark and ragged cloak
And carries a bright lamp so common folk
Will steer away: his spirit's not to share.
But someone gave the Hermit's light its birth,
And someone put bright jewels in the earth.

19

The child walked down the corridor one day;
The door at one end small, at the other, large.
Alone, despite her status as the charge
Of two fond parents, each with its own way
Of viewing things, each with a fund of thoughts
On various subjects, and from various books
(Some thoughts unwieldy, some just specks and orts
Though neither entertained pale djinns or spooks).
She travelled books herself; she learned to write;
She mixed together all the tastes she knew,
Boiled them all down to the last, best - the few.
Time passed. At length the child's long evening
waned.
Only the world she'd brought to life remained.

20

A certain lack of preaching might confuse
Enquirers when they mix at first with Friends:
Quakers do not speak out, but rather choose
To split with those who preach for worldly ends,
In steeple-houses full of arty types
Of story-telling; statues, tombs and glass -
Designed to teach the faithful as they pass
How steel-clad martial tigers change their stripes,
(Having pursued the Muslims in crusades)
And hope to storm high Heaven's palisades.
In Paradise, there dwells equality.
One cannot speak, but feel, the mystery.

21

Tall as my good left hand, pale pink and gold
Topped by a handle, armed with teeth inside
It stands, complete with drawer. I was not told
About this curious birthday gift, and tried
To think it pleasant; what I'd always lacked,
Whilst also trying to think how my right claw
Could operate the thing, once its brass maw
Was packed with beans, its shapely funnel stacked.
Not many things cannot be used by me:
Huge broadsheet newspapers that flail about,
Jars where the little button won't pop out
And manual coffee grinders - give me tea!
(But in that awkward grating is the sound
Of friendship, fragrant as the beans, fresh-ground.)

22

As worship finished, the two young boys kissed:
Two students, dressed in leather, sitting close,
Backs to the window, kissed - I nearly missed
The incident - it seemed like one of those
Short kisses giving promise of much more
To be enacted once they were alone
(The bed, the disconnected telephone,
The pillows quickly thrown onto the floor).
This is a love that has a horrid wood
To cross before its cottage can be reached:
A wood of trees that rooted when men preached
That heretics in love forswore all good.
But these young lovers love in innocence:
I wish them (Quaker) Whitman's confidence.

23 (The Arnolfini Wedding)

They stand before us, in their curious shoes,
Stiff poses, covered heads inside the house,
Married, but keeping close the happy news
Herr pious rat and his demure *vrouw* mouse.
A column of cool darkness, his large eyes
Stray to her green earth-mother looking gown;
Fat with a baby, or too many pies,
Her eyes bright devils that she must cast down.
The Flemish bourgeois boom, the moment when
The sober businessman chose something drab;
The peacock's colours fled to the new pea-hen:
Mercutio died, who painted bright Queen Mab:
So he will doff plain pattens before bed,
And she'll cast off jewelled slippers of deep red.

24

The child, Miranda, made the difference
To Prosper, as he mounted the strange beach
Of that lone island where he'd soon dispense
Justice, and the ways of cities - teach
The brutal monster, wayward apparitions.
Without Miranda to give motive, he'd
Have taken up old habits, seen no need
To trap and scare the wayward politicians.
Once I was cast away, inside my head:
Soon I began to hate all living things;
The daughter chirruping, the bird that sings,
Drove me to Bedlam, living but half dead.
Against these feelings I had small defence:
The child, Miranda, made the difference.

25 (Arnolfini Wedding II)

One year along, the stout maid dusts the frame
Of the strange picture by that man Van Eyck.
The bedroom and its fitments are the same,
But oh, the picture's subjects grow unlike.
No stand-in for a mirror, the oil shows
A stealthy transformation that will strike
The watcher who observes life's curious twists.
Once a bland puff-fish, she grows like a pike:
Too much *geneva* softens his sharp face.
The 'master of the house' cannot resolve
Their money problems - she stands in his place
And, unrespected, watches marks dissolve.
One thing that might remind them of their start,
The picture, stays inscrutable as art.

26

After three boyfriends, Jenny is depressed
(They always leave her for much younger types).
Lenny, who felt so lonely and distressed
Cheers up and paints his room in candy stripes.
All through the rooms, the troubled of the earth
Wade through their problems, weigh up death and birth,
Get stuck, then fish around for the right key
And visit Gabe for a strong cup of tea.
Gabe, the tall landlord, lives below the street
And looks up through the area to view
The passing mortals (or at least their feet).
Strange that to him each day seems yellow, new.
Alone, he checks the ceilings of the rooms:
Soars up, and clears the cobwebs with his plumes.

27

Aunt Sarah's running in a marathon,
Riding a bike, flying a solo plane;
She goes out walking in the pouring rain
Without the thinnest kind of raincoat on.
Her children are alarmed at her new wheels:
A giant Harley-Davison she rides
Down all the deadly Welsh Wales mountainsides,
To younger residents' despairing squeals.
She wears good make-up, but is imprecise
And sometimes looks like Dietrich's raddled ghost.
Her daughter, (forty) when they meet, is ice;
Of all the biker gangs, her mum's the toast.
The daughter is the thoughtless one, I fear:
While Sarah gets more serious every year.

28

Nearly ten years of teaching to those ranks
Of children, ten to sixteen, girls and boys:
A worrying job which earns one little thanks
And fills the head with real, or inner, noise.
You will have heard that in this sceptered isle
Too many finish school without the trick
Of reading properly; or writing thick
Uneven letters in an infant style:
Worse, many lack the basic human skills
For talking simply, calmly, with concern.
Perhaps, by sitting close, some child did learn
From me, the art of tilting at windmills.
The sanguine being drained to the last drop,
My melancholy part knew when to stop.

29

So much is written, painted, stored away;
We English keep our art so close to home,
Waiting, I suppose, until the fated day
Strangers shall finger every scroll or tome,
After our deaths, consigning them to burn.
Pale water-colours, oils, a clay maquette,
Enclosed in fire's convenient oubliette:
And from these things, there was so much to learn -
How paper might last longer than the hand
That wrote upon it once; some trivial note,
Of Fox's *Journal*, or tract Nayler wrote,
That lives in Quaker minds in every land.
If God has function here, then it is this:
He must remember us, for we are his.

30

Irt-Iw, slim Egyptian girl, exposed
In her pale coffin, given a thick coat
Of shiny varnish, unwrapped, unopposed;
Hands roughly crossed beneath her withered throat.
Enough survives, for me to clothe in flesh,
Of bones that nearly tear the tent of skin,
To see a girl who'd surely flourish in
Our time, when twenty plus avoids fate's mesh.
Yet, the insulting fact of this display,
This leather silhouette, this shameful sight
In such a seat of learning would propel
Irt-Iw upon her ancient, barge-borne flight
Back to Osiris' heaven, or his hell.
Our recent, English dead lie unexposed:
Old Africans don't count, it is supposed.

31

The island, and old Ithaca provide
Similar pleasures for the sensual sort.
If you had stayed at home, no friend had died
By Ilium, by Hector's javelin caught.
Penelope does not require white scars
To cherish your brown hero's body, Greek:
She'd rather not watch suitors growing sleek;
Turn your respect *to* Venus, and *from* Mars.
Let dark Calypso keep you on her strand,
Take off your armour's final pieces now;
Leave your triumphant comeback tour unplanned
And stargaze from your beached boat's jutting prow.
Neglect to sample the sour fruits of war
Stay on Calypso's island one day more.

32

They hang around on corners, like bad news,
In baseball caps and brand-new training shoes.
They shout from time to time, and sometimes strike
Each other's arms, the better to misuse
Whatever hints of boyish love they choose.
They've sprayed each wall and pilfered every bike,
And answer questions with fine-tuned replies.
They try to mitigate their human face
With jutting chins and all-evading eyes.
They lure young girls with danger, and reward
Their loves with trips to passion's darkest place
(Those single mums one sees, so much deplored.)
In any city, seek these lads - you'll find
Such monsters lurking only in your mind.

33

The boy fought madly with his jumper, till
His head appeared above its formal blue.
The teacher cried out - cut-glass, pointed, shrill,
'Delroy, I must explain a thing to you:
In England, we all put our little heads
Out through the neck-hole, then search out the arms.'
Delroy was startled: so, the clustered beds,
Jamaican patois, postcards of green palms
That filled his home, made it a nation state!
That run-down Croydon avenue now held
Adventure; opportunities: if late
For school he'd claim a border-guard had yelled:
'Take care in that strange country's curious maze,
Where clothes are donned in unimagined ways.'

34

They asked themselves, what lies beyond this wall?
They picked a hole and gazed into the murk.
They'd not expected anything at all:
To make an entrance was their morning's work.
Like Carter and Carnarvon they gazed in
And sensed a dark, arched space, with rusty air.
After a moment they could all begin
To recognise the badness that was there.
Old leg-irons lay strewn about the floor:
A ball and chain lay, like an iron sperm.
Black, crusted brackets reinforced the door...
The arch had been a prison for a term,
And Betsy Fry had come to visit twice,
Offering comfort in her God's advice.

35

Offering comfort in his God's advice,
He walked about the country unopposed
By Christian people; but those over-nice
In matters of dry doctrine soon supposed
He was a danger, and pitched everything
They could against him: law and lawlessness;
Street-fiddlers to drown out his will to sing,
Villains with clubs, and such unmanliness...
New laws were minted, old ones brought to light,
Points stretched, the Bible scoured for likely traps;
While civil war fed fat the wheeling kite.
The Quakers' spread was plotted on broad maps...
But nothing can prevent the tender word,
Wherever it is felt, and truly heard.

36

Wherever it is felt and truly heard,
His story provokes pity and not hate.
As his immortal status was conferred,
The autumn of his life was confiscate.
Converted 'at the plough' he soon set out
To find the inspiration that he sought.
Trapped in a Roundhead carapace of fear
He quartermastered, marched, preached hard and
fought.
Later, the hosts of peace so flocked to hear,
His strong brown head was turned, and a sad fate
Awaited him at Bristol's city gate.
To be like Jesus, for a Christian Friend,
Is all that really matters in the end.

37

Is all that really matters in the end
The need to live a truly blameless life,
Bathed in the gentle speech of Friend to Friend
Mourned by fond children, and a loving wife?
Penn's *Fruits of Solitude* was not produced
To force new Quakers into monasteries,
But warned Friends how to shun a life traduced
By outer or by inner enemies;
Pursuing blameless trades for virtue's sake,
In Pennsylvania, where, one has to say
The Quaker Eden's brilliance gave way
To the hangman's rope: the Garden's plaited snake.
Thus our first parents, when, before the Fall,
They asked themselves, 'What lies behind this wall?'

38

The war was over, roughly twenty years:
Recovery had renewed the English state;
The nation's caring tissue wiped all tears,
And rescued the last poor from their poor fate.
(That is at least the general picture, held
In mind by many liberal advocates.
A certain decade virtually dispelled
This hope, and clung to what hard cash dictates.)
Extracted from a crumbling Tudor pile
The Parish Church School pupils fondly eyed
Ten glass shoe-boxes in the modern style;
Where prejudices could be set aside,
And all the Empire's children could rejoice
To sing together with one faltering voice.

39

To sing together with one faltering voice,
The choir stood up and shuffled its small feet.
It seemed to hesitate, then made the choice
To belt out some old hymn: quite incomplete
The sound reached me: a sort of whispering.
When someone turned the record up at home,
Then I could hear Nat Cole, Sinatra, sing;
But elsewhere all was dumb, my mind would roam...
My deafness would resolve itself at length,
The blockages dissolve themselves, or move;
Old boxes of precocious drawings prove
That once my visual sense was a great strength.
My soundless entertainment was to think;
Like Captain Cook, lost on a new world's brink.

40

Like Captain Cook, lost on a new world's brink,
I lifted the cigar up to my lips.
Keen to remove the troubling need to think
I poured the gin and took two nervous sips.
I knew she would be soft and do no harm,
But conversation I did not expect;
Winter or summer, the first girl was warm -
Helplessly, I entered love's elect.
Taken together, all these drugs can be
Disastrous - to mix good, and worthless things
Can soon obscure the good which first we see.
Drink sends true love to sleep and crops its wings:
The body has its proper opiates,
Lodged in a city poison infiltrates.

41

Lodged in a city poison infiltrates
Within the quarter of profound delight
Is Simpleness: a figure the world hates
And tries to hide from artificial light.
Beyond her pale, people in search of joy
Delight in buying things they cannot own.
(The child who fills his room with every toy
Is trapped by them, and must play on alone.)
Poor stricken ships, in our seafaring past
Have sunk themselves to gain a stretch of sand
Beside a reef; but watch them - at long last
All is reclaimed by water's gradual hand.
A costly treasure on a coral perch,
The atom-sub becomes the salmon's church.

42

The atom-sub becomes the salmon's church;
He knows as little as we humans know
What should transpire if the dark thing should lurch
Sideways, and break up on the rocks below.
The fuel rods' thin containment, eaten through
By years of saline water, might erupt,
A soup bowl, dropped and shattered, helpless, spew
Its radiation, and make all corrupt.
Sometimes I hope the world's worst problems now
Might be the heritage that's left behind
And that our greatest questions should be how
To deal with all the debris we will find
Of those last days, when strength led to more fears,
And the war was over roughly twenty years.

Notes to Some of the Sonnets

5. The sonnet refers to James Nayler, the controversial early Quaker and older contemporary of George Fox. See my *Life and Times of James Nayler, the 'Quaker Jesus'*.

6. The sonnet compares North-European Paganism of the type some would like to see revived with Christianity which, like Islam and Judaism, was born from a dry place.

8. Based on the old story of a Quaker Meeting for Worship in America where a venomous snake was seen on a roof-beam above the Friends.

9. Based on my one experience of a visit to a Spiritualist church, in the 1970s.

11. This sonnet recounts my various physical flaws.

16. Both the Friends in Christ and the Quakers of Fritchley in Yorkshire were Quaker groups unconnected to mainstream Quakerism in the UK.

17. The Hierophant and the Hermit mentioned here are depicted on tarot cards.

21. More about my physical drawbacks: this time my deformed right hand.

22. Based on an occasion when two gay men kissed at the end of Meeting for Worship, instead of shaking hands. The American poet Walt Whitman was gay, and had a Quaker mother.

23. The reader who does not know Van Eyck's painting *The Arnolfini Wedding* really should look it up or go and see it in the National Gallery in London.

24. Having a daughter called Miranda, one can sometimes imagine one is Prospero – both of these characters appear in *The Tempest* by William Shakespeare.

25. 'Geneva' is a Dutch alcoholic drink.

26. 'Dietrich' is the German singer and actress Marlene Dietrich.

28. The last two lines reference the doctrine of the humours, whereby the body is thought to be made up of blood, bile, black bile (melancholy) and phlegm.

30. Irt-Iw is an unwrapped ancient Egyptian mummy once shown naked in a museum in Newcastle-upon-Tyne. Last time I visited her, she was more respectfully displayed.

31. Based on Ulysses' dilemma in Homer's Odyssey. Should he choose love and idleness on Calypso's island, or love and war back home in Ithaca?

33. Based on an incident I remember from primary school. A teacher explained to a West Indian boy how we put jumpers on *in this country*.

34. Refers to the discovery of the tomb of Tutankhamen and the more recent re-discovery of a cell from the old Durham House of Correction, which was visited by the Quaker prison reformer Elizabeth Fry. Sonnets 34-37 form a 'crown of sonnets', with each last line repeated as the first line of the next poem, and the first line of 34 repeated as the last line of 37.

35. George Fox.

36. Based on the life of James Nayler.

37. Line 12 refers to the fact that there was hanging in William's Penn's Quaker Paradise, Pennsylvania.

38. Begins another crown of sonnets.

39. Refers to another health problem: infantile deafness.

42. Based on the true story of an atomic submarine, complete with nuclear warheads, that sank and could not be recovered.

For free downloads and more from the Langley Press, please visit our website at: http://tinyurl.com/lpdirect

Printed in Great Britain
by Amazon

62570214R00033